The Gospel of Radiance

New and Selected Poems

by

Nick LeForce

Published by

Inner Works
2580 W El Camino Ave. Unit 13103
Sacramento, CA 95833

Cover Art by
Nick LeForce

Devotion

The Gospel of Radiance
Is devoted to all seekers of the light

and

To all those who identify as SBNR:
Spiritual But Not Religious

Gospel Of Radiance
Table Of Contents

Preface

Despite the title, this is not a religious text. It is not a declaration of truth. It is a book of poetry. For whatever reason, the imagery and iconography of religious symbolism and spiritual metaphor often inspire me. I have always felt a strong sense of the numinous, that everything is alive and imbued with spirit. I often feel as if other-worldly presences, angels if you wish, hover on the periphery of my awareness. But I am also a pragmatist and recognize that these mystical experiences may simply be constructs of my overly active imagination. As a practicing hypnotherapist, I know the magic power of the unconscious to organize perception, thought, and sensation into meaningful expressions that serve to help us manage life and understand how we might relate to a vast and incomprehensible world.

I resisted the urge to include religious symbols or words in my poetry for years. I remember the first time the word God appeared in a poem. At first, I tried to use synonyms, but they did not seem right and, with trepidation and a rampant heart, I finally put it on the page, staring at it for several minutes with a mix of excitement and dread. Until very recently, I continued to feel awkward including words and images associated with spiritual traditions or religious canon. But they were coming to me with greater frequency and with increasing welcome on my part. The floodgates opened when the phrase that serves as the title of this book, *The Gospel of Radiance*, showed up in a line of poetry. In that moment, I decided to drop the hesitation and give my full blessing to these intuitions, curious where they would lead me. Despite this newfound welcome, I am clear that I will not run off and get baptized or join a monastery or profess a particular faith.

This work is a testament of my own wavering faith in a greater intelligence. It is primarily a faith in the process of *divining*, of opening a channel through which I access and co-create poetry. The often surprising arrival of spiritual symbolism and religious imagery, and my resistance to it, serves as my evidence that I am in touch with something beyond my conscious awareness and that a greater intelligence is speaking through me. Of course, whatever the source and however it arrives, the words are still written by my hand and spoken by my mouth. On the one hand, I cannot take credit for the wisdom. On the other hand, I must take responsibility for the content. It is not my intention to mock, offend, or disrespect anyone's faith. These poems reflect my own imaginal landscape and are not meant to be an indictment of any belief system. They do not call for a conversion to any faith. Read it for entertainment, or as an invitation to ponder and grapple with your own relationship with spirituality and how faith works in your own life.

In 2013, I wrote *This Is Poetry,* my first poem that clearly and dramatically crossed the boundary to step firmly on spiritual ground. It was previously published in my 3rd book of poetry, *Divine Whispering.* I offer it here because it best describes the relationship between poetry and spirituality for me and to invite you, my dear reader, to use this work as a portal to the precious treasure within you.

This Is Poetry

Poetry is the Divine whispering secrets in your ear.
Spoken in the Mother-tongue, the ancient language
of sounds that synchronize the soul
and harmonize the heart.

To your ear it will be sweet nothings
and the feeling that you are loved.

Poetry is the lightest touch from the longed-for lover,
the ever-so-slight stroke of fingers along
the nape of your neck, electric and tingling,
that lights up all your senses and
awakens your yearning to be complete.

Poetry is the portal to the precious treasure within you:
the passageway to your highest purpose and
deepest passion, the doorway to your destiny
and the future to which you have always belonged.

And the key to all poetry is the heart.

Every word you take into your heart will take you
to all this and beyond to what cannot be named or numbered.

Each sound you turn over and over in your heart
will, in time, turn up the secrets of your own Divine Soul.

Then, if you lend your whispered voice to the Mother-Tongue,
the Divine will echo through you across time:

In the beginning was the word
and the word was with God.
This is poetry.

How To Read This Book

This book is a collection of new and selected poems written along the way on the path of my surrender to spiritual imagery and religious references that appeared in my poetry. Most of the poems were written in 2018 and 2019 and a few were selected from earlier collections that served a role in the evolution of my relationship to the divine. There is no logical sequence to the poems and you can read them in any order. In the process of collection, I realized that the poems could be loosely organized into five sections. Each section has a brief introduction and an initial poem that seemed to capture the section's primary concern. The sections are as follows:

Abandon and Surrender: Poems that explore the theme of relinquishing the hold on life and the way life should be and surrendering to a greater will.

Sacred and Secular: Poems about developing and maintaining an attitude toward life as sacred in a secular world.

Prayers and Blessings: Poems that explore the power of prayer and the beauty of blessing in living well.

Heaven and Earth: Poems that relate to the topic of being a spirit in a physical body and living in a material world.

Gods and Guides: Poems about or with references to God or spiritual guides, specific mythological beings, and prophets.

I have a practice of writing letters to my future self. I select a date on the calendar and then I write a letter in a notes application called Evernote with a reminder to read it on the selected date. One such letter referred to becoming a "holy man," a notion that completely baffled and frightened me because It seemed too lofty a goal and too far from the life I lived. Over the years, I have written about this idea and what it might actually mean to me and how it might work in my life. The **Addendum** includes a selection of writing about becoming a holy man, including the original "letter to my future self" and the "reply" from my future self that first referenced this idea.

Finally, there is a **Notes** section that gives background and commentary on some of the poems included in this collection.

The Gospel of Radiance

Introduction

If I were to adhere to any "religious" orientation, it would likely be a stream of Buddhism. Buddhist philosophy and practices seem the most open and amenable to other ways of thinking and being in life than other spiritual traditions of which I am aware. The Buddha, or what some might consider Buddhist influence, appears in many of my poems. Christianity, however, is the dominant religious orientation of my culture. I am not a Christian. I am not a believer in the resurrection of Jesus. I have never been baptized. I have not attended any Church as a member, although Church's of all kinds intrigue me. I take the miraculous stories from the old and new testament as metaphors for a spiritual journey. I know this risks blasphemy in the eyes of some. To me, any dogma that is a closed set, that does not tolerate outside ideas, or that considers non-believers infidels or sinners, cannot represent a living God. To add to my blasphemy, I cannot even say with confidence that there is an entity or force that we might call "God."

A core ingredient in "right relationship" with the one's Self and with life is openness to what flows through us. I recall the first time I read the Gospel of Thomas, the gnostic gospel that I found most illuminating, because the core message is about how we relate to our own inner world. Early on in the text, there is a quote that profoundly affected me: "If you bring forth what is within you, what you bring forth will save you. If you do not bring forth what is within you, what you do not bring forth will destroy you." The truth of this and the practice of living it has been a lifelong journey for me. And this book is a step in that journey, a step toward living in the world as a spirit with my heart open to the flow of life through me.

I know my heart is open when something comes from the inner depths that truly surprises me, that often rattles my cage, and that sometimes challenges my stronghold on the familiar life or my sense of life as it should be. One such incident occurred when I was writing a letter to my future self, a practice I have exercised over the past several years, in the arrival of a line instructing me, "to turn your life over to God and become a holy man." I initially resisted this idea, as usual, refusing to write it until I realized that to do so would cut the flow. As mentioned earlier, I was not raised religious and I never took formal religious training, except for Westernized versions of "Shamanism" as practiced by the Navajo, Toltec, and Inca traditions. So, I have no claim to legitimacy as a holy man.

"If you bring forth what is within you, what you bring forth will save you. If you do not bring forth what is within you, what you do not bring forth will destroy you."

--The Gospel of Thomas

I cannot say that I have the answer to what this means or that I will achieve whatever my unconscious mind or the guiding presence was trying to convey by this image. I have spent many hours exploring why this line would come to me in my writing because such an identity seems so elevated compared to the way I live my life. The origin of the word holy can be traced back to mean "whole" and to the same root word for "health." It was originally used to mean "that which must be preserved whole or intact; that which must not to be violated." The late priest/poet/ philosopher John O'Donoghue said, "to be holy is to be able to be inner and to be able to rest in the house of belonging…" I certainly qualify for the first half of that definition because I have devoted my life to exploring the inner landscape. To me, this means I am a holy man to the degree that I explore my own undiscovered country and live in my own heartland.

The second part of O' Donahue's definition, to "rest in the house of belonging," cuts to the core issue of my life. I have always felt myself to be a misfit, living just far enough outside the norm to be an outsider in society but still close enough to be seen and, ideally, to be

10

loved. There are times when I think I have achieved this and there are other times when I feel the sting of distance between myself and others. Now that I am divorced, having only a few friends nearby, and many others who live in faraway places and with whom I only have periodic contact, I have mostly resigned myself to living a singular life. This makes it easier for me, in some ways, to make myself holy: that is to treat my "Self" as something "that must be preserved whole or intact" and protect my "Self" from "being violated."

This book is about the journey to find a place of belonging as a spirit in the world. It is about finding and creating the "right relationship" with oneself and with life. In many ways, it is a journey without a destination, because it is a process of perpetual arrival. We are each granted a divine spark, a light that is ours to shine. The word "gospel" is actually a truncated version of "god spell," which itself was a misspoken version of "good spell," or good story. *The Gospel of Radiance* is the story of returning to one's light, of finding the courage and desire to shine despite the challenges of life and the condemnation of others. It is what we were made to do. Even the smallest stars shine as brightly as they can without concern for how their light compares to others and even if their glow is absorbed in the radiance of greater stars. Look at our own sun, beaming out in all directions, far from grand in size and scope and residing on the outskirts of the Milky Way, surrounded by billions of bigger, brighter brethren. Yet it has produced this earthly gem and us too, who have the power to appreciate it. We do not know what our light might give rise to and that is why we must shine as brightly as we can.

Light

Light is the one thing
that cannot see itself
because it is always
traveling ahead
of its own reflection,
always pushing the edge,
always transforming
beyond into the moment.

As spirit, you
are made of light,
and you can never
truly know yourself
because all reflection
is outdated.

You have already
gone beyond
where you were,
you are already
breaking new ground.

The best you can do
is ride the wave
of your life,
eyes open and
heart thrilled,
with awe and wonder
at the new world
you participate
in creating,
the beyond you are
transforming, even now,
into this moment.

The Gospel of Radiance

Abandon & Surrender

All religions share a single premise: that we are part of something greater than ourselves. Religions differ with regard to what that "greater-ness" is composed of and how we should or could relate to it, with, perhaps, one common ingredient: that the "greater-ness" is a mystery beyond our comprehension requiring a humbling attitude of respect and reverence. Despite our advances in technology and the way we have shaped the world to our comfort, we are still at the mercy of greater forces. The word "religion" is likely derived from the latin "relegare," which means "to bind fast" and was originally used to describe a "bond between humans and gods." Many religions include references to some form of promise, agreement or covenant that followers must keep in order to remain in the favor of the gods or that gods extend to humans who follow them. The bond generally includes two essential acts: abandoning worldly aspirations and surrendering to a greater will. The highest form of this abandonment and surrender occurs in the context of a cloistered or monastic life. The poems in this section explore the theme of relinquishing our own dictates about the way life should be and surrendering to a greater will.

Down To The Bone

Picking at it over and over again,
wondering: will it end at thigh or rib?
Or something without a name—
a missing link in a line
that leads back to apes and to angels.
And, once found, fills the gaps, answers all the questions
that we have chewed on for years.

I tell myself over and over again,
"I have no need of these things."
No need to count sheets through the shredder
or bags full of memories put in garbage bins
or trunk–filled trips to Goodwill,
though every item held a piece of me
hostage, abandoned. Scattered now to the world—

the ashes of loved ones finally freed.

At last laying the past to rest
for we have lives to live and life
will pick at us over and over again
until we feel it clean through to the bone
and know ourselves as apes and as angels
and as something without a name.

The Wonder Is In You

If air is the element of lung,
then why are you short of breath?
And water is the element of gut,
then why are you so thirsty?

If the wonder is not in you,
having crawled from sea to sky,
then why do you kiss the ground
after it has shaken?

Your cup is full,
but trembling, you spill it
and then curse the gods
for your misfortune.

In anger, you break faith,
smash the idols and then
you look down and see
shards of a broken mirror.

A gift is given to you, but
you don't believe it is yours.
Then one day you trip over it
and your heart is broken.

This is what it means to be human,
foolish, malcontented, wanting it all.
Earth is your element and it
is hard and unforgiving.

But as long as the wonder is in you,
you will still kiss the ground
after you fall.

Self-Indulgence

OK, I admit it, nothing grabs me.
I've been standing here with the lightning pole
ready for inspiration, but the clouds break

and the sun shines through and I am left
longing to be kissed by some Disney
dream angel in the middle of the night.

I want to give you God, but I keep
revving the engine with trash talk
and then I pop the bottle at the start.

I want to dazzle you, sweep your heart up
in my hands, make you sit on the edge of
your chair, awestruck and eager for every word.

You are at the heart of my silly, extravagant
self-indulgence because everything I do,
I do for you.

The Shadow Of Your Silence

It's backbreaking work,
leveraging joy over everything.

Now that the shelves sparkle
and the empty spaces sigh with relief,
I can see another future: One with
room enough for love to flourish.

My biggest gamble is putting
the whole matter in the hands of God.

The ante is high, and I'm all in,
but I don't know what the stakes are.
I tell myself, "It's OK because
I've got nothing to lose."

I've already lived a lifetime
in the shadow of your silence.

If faith is an investment, then
I want to get real dividends, not just
creative accounting to show a prophet
on the bottom line. I say a ritual prayer,

mouthing the words silently while
I leverage joy over your silence.

Radical Acceptance

When I became a window,
flung open, I was not prepared
for the blast.

The struggle to catch anything
would blow me over. I had to
let it go.

The movie had 1 billion
frames per second,
flooding through with
disjointed images,
disparate scenes,
a jumble of mismatched
puzzle pieces and half-told stories,
all streaming through me.

I watched it blur by. Occasionally,
I rapid tracked the passing bits
and my head shook back
and forth until I noticed
I was secretly saying "No."

To really let go, I needed
the radical acceptance
of the frame. I needed
a transparency of eye.
I needed love to hold me
back from myself.

Then I felt it! The world,
the entire universe,
becoming divine as it
passed through me.

Sieve

Before I was burned,
I did not believe in fire.

I was spared the slap of reality.
I never needed to heal the welts
from the whip of love.

My life was easy. "Blessed," you may say.
Kept from death, I never saw maggots
feed on the flesh of transformation.

My eyes were clean. The stains
on my soul were far too small
to warrant a hero's medal.

Yet here I am, standing on privilege,
as if I have a right to the holy staff.
I am too weak a vessel for the divine.
It leaks out of me like a sieve
and the flow never ends.

After years closing the lid,
patching up the holes,
I've lost interest in resistance.
I know it will shatter me.
But I say, "bring it on,"
because, deep down,
I know I will not
believe in the light
until it blinds me.

Refuse The Fig Leaf

It's all the same at the end of the day.

One more ticked off on the calendar of days
and we still do not know how to escape
our own equivocation.

We don't know when it ends
or how the numbering of our days
add up to a life.

Even though we have memories
stretching back into the shadows
and a bright sun on the next horizon,

time still marches on and tramples
yesterday's truths into dust.

Now it seems all of those we chastised
for living out loud had it right all along.

Maybe this is why poets skirt the outer edge,
run ninja routines in the night and steal
fruit from the forbidden tree.

When they are cast out,
they refuse to wear the fig leaf.
When arrested, they say:
"only our nakedness
can save us now."

Everything Gives Way

The wise man said, "everything gives way."

I wasn't sure if I heard it right
and repeated it back to him.

He simply nodded his head and told me
it was the question I did not ask.

I am sure it is one of those riddles, a koan,
meant to crack open the doors of perception
and rain revelation into the heart, like,
"can a dog with Buddha nature clap with one hand?"
or "how can you carry beauty across the river
with an empty cup full of taboo tea and
a hungry tiger at your back?"

I could not tell him the question I didn't ask
because it felt like bathwater draining out of the tub when a door
opens to another world.
I heard a voice in the distance forecasting rain,
heavy at times, with a chance of flash floods.

The wise man laughed and instructed me,
"Take heart," as if this solved the equation
and then he repeated his mantra,
"Everything gives way."

Suddenly, I know the question I didn't ask
completes that sentence with "to what?"
And the answer in his equation
floods me with joy.

Waiting For A Sign

If this poem is meant to say,
"no hero will save you,"
it is because the wait
for a sign is an open book.

If God has a mouth, then
it is the place from which
you came into and will go
out of this world.

If this poem is meant to say,
"the wait is over," it is
because your whole life
is a word from that mouth.

The Gospel Of Radiance

I booked a dream before I boarded, flush
with excitement for the adventure I imagined.

There were storms on the high passage,
unanticipated delays, detours that
wound through dark lands.

Complaints filled the mouths
of weary wanderers and I fell in step,
wanting to belong. I caught myself
painting the walls with sour grapes
when I wanted the wine of life.

I can't tell you what happens to
digitized dreams when the computer
crashes, but I know the clutch of hollowness
in a single, one-letter step from loss to lost.

If the hate lives in me, it doesn't matter
where I point the finger. The bitter heart
is not the home of my lord.

The first point of reference is locating
the arrow on the map that says "you are here."

When you realize every elsewhere, even
the alluring one right before your eyes,
is a dream, you can take the second
one-letter step from live to love.
This is the whole message in
"The Gospel of Radiance."

Life Before God

Who has not
worked their fingers
to the bone
for a lost cause,
traded their
hard-earned cash
for what cannot
be bought or sold?

We only carry
our lives on
our backs
so the weight of it
will bring us
to our knees
and then we
bow down,
laying our life
at your feet.

Blemish

It's not so easy to rise
into our greatness
after all the years
molding ourselves
into the shape of shame.

If beauty is without blemish,
how can the the hole in our hearts
be the reed through which
God makes music?

Why not become the instrument?

Let the changing shape of you
form another note as God plays,
through you, the love song of your life.

When You Are A Stranger

When you are a stranger,
everyone around you is a teacher.

Little lessons learned by observation:
how to behave at the dinner table;
how to negotiate the subway turnstile;
how to step through the crowd;
how to shape oneself in or to a world
that has its own relentless demands.

A small act can ignite imagination
and open the door to a life lived.

It's easy to slip through the tiny crack
into something that has waited quietly
inside, like evening primrose and
moonflowers, blossoming in the dark
where others do not tread.

With gentle resolve, you can feel your way
into the skin, shape yourself into another,
and your mind can enter the foreign temple.

If you bow before the strange god,
dropping your intemperance, you will
be given a dip in the holy water
and gifted another fleeting, fragile life,
with all its disappointment and desire,
slipping through you, leaving behind
a little gift for you to love even though
you may never fully understand what it is.

Practice

There is a calm,
at the core of our being
that remains steady
despite the weather of our day
or the storms of our lives

This is the place
that remains true to
the unanswered question
that does not rush
to completion because
we have yet to live it
into an answer

The soul seeking
its own expression
welcomes the weather
as an invitation
to shape a reply
that serves our thriving

Learning to find
and trust this place
is the practice
of a lifetime

Karmic Carousel

See how everything is going to hell.
I think God is getting old. He's more
concerned about his bucket list
than a puny little planet where
his own image can't bear itself.

Top of the list: appear
as a giant illuminated talking head,
simultaneously, in all the temples
around the world and say, "Gotcha!"

Then, he'll sit back and watch. He's sure
we will go ballistic. It would be
the perfect season finale and
undoubtably kick-up his ratings.

Yes, I am sure he's getting old.
So, what should we give him?

I'm tired of the undying devotion thing
that he claims is his due despite
the divorce papers. He also says
"the elk loves the wolf before the kill."

He was always better at math,
so I take his word for it, baring
my neck to him. If I prove him wrong,
I win and I'm off the karmic carousel.
If he wins, I want to come back
as a koala bear.

The Gospel of Radiance

Sacred & Secular

To me, spirituality is not adherence to a particular creed but an attitude of reverence toward life. It is easy to fall into routines and take our life, and the people and things in it, for granted. When we do, they become aspects of the everyday world and recede into the background of our awareness. We treat them as 'secular,' which simply means "of this world," of the mundane, day-to-day, earthly world. The word 'sacred' comes from the Latin root meaning "to set apart," to consecrate, or to make holy. In other words, we make things holy by how we hold them in our hearts. The poems in this section celebrate that breathtaking view of life as holy and recognize that we all must dance this dance between the mundane and the magical.

Walk In Sacred Space

Let your feet be guided by open spaces,
your eyes by soulful truth,
your ears by whispered wisdom,
and you will walk in sacred space
throughout the day.

Lumbering Angels

We are lumbering angels on the earth
laden with wings we do not know
how to use or refuse to work.

We live our lives with frightened eyes
making enemies of each other.
We put our hopes in our head
and in our weapons of mass destruction
keeping our demons at a distance
so we will not have to dance with them
in the dead of the night.

Our wings shall be our burden,
a heavy cloak we wrap around ourselves
covering our hearts, until we find our lightness
and learn our place on the planet.

Because the highest in us lives
in our hearts and not our heads,
in our compassion and not our cunning.

And it takes two wings to lift us.
We will never truly soar until
the wing of our humanity equals
the wing of our divinity.

Dharma

Dharma is a river that runs both ways,
a light turned in on itself, a footbridge
you walk everyday and never cross.

In the mountain of the heart,
there is a temple you cannot see.
To get there is to cross the uncrossable bridge
and to worship there is to live the dharma.

If you ask how, those who know will tell you
"Don't look to where the finger is pointing.
Be the source of the light."

Forbidden Fruit

Is there still a fruit forbidden to us?
Perhaps it is the holy seed of life.
Does DNA stand for "Do Not Alter?"

Somewhere, God could be screaming,
"don't touch," and we have forgotten
how to listen. But who can we blame?

If we were made in His likeness,
then isn't our defiance itself divine?
I have a new theory: perhaps God

made us in his image because
he could no longer stand himself.
We are just like him in that regard.

How boring to be god: to be one
and everything, all seeing, all knowing
and all powerful, to be the one who

can suffer an eternity of loneliness.
Don't pray to god, pray for god.
It may be the only prayer we can hear.

——

P.S.: God did not punish us
for eating from the tree of knowledge.
Our exile, like his, is self-imposed.

Native Tongue

Suddenly I
remember
my native
tongue,
the language
of beauty,
spoken with
out faces
or names and
I question
my origins:

was I adopted
by the world?

Because I've
always had
stars in my eyes.

I've always
worn this
alien skin
with strange
delight.

I've always
tried my best
to weave the world
into wonder and
wander the world
witnessing miracles
one after another.

Animal Eyes

To look at the world
with animal eyes
is to see it as it is.

Seeing, hearing, and feeling
it all in a wordless silence that
links sense to sensations
of desire and fear.

Without language to connect the dots,
the world is isolated observations,
a dispersed group of islands
in a vast and mysterious sea.

With animal sense, we see the wall,
the color blue, and know the direction left;
but we cannot calculate: "left of the blue wall."

This capacity to layer abstractions
in linked associations that map the world
is what funds our human magic.

It allows us to navigate by the stars
and to make sense of things
in patterns we can name.

We sing songs to gods unseen,
count grains of sand on distant shores.

We cast footprints in the lunar dust,
and leave our littered remains
on the only place we can call home.

I Am The Fool

I am the fool,
walking on air,
eyes cast
to the stars,
a beggar's bag
on my shoulders
and a flower
in my hand,
my winged heart
soaring to God,
while the world
to which I belong
turns under my feet,
offering me
everything.

No Excuse For Light

There is no excuse for light.
Quick to give and unapologetic,
few realize how easily it is bent.

Cat eyes perceive the truth
we have forgotten because
we no longer go slow enough
to fall in love with faulty things.

We complain to the clouds
for hiding the sun until
they pour the colors of sunset
over our mesmerized hearts.

Then we sleep again,
rising to the world without
the courtesy of a bow.

How can we learn to see
when the slit in our feral eye
is too narrow to let in the light?

But when we are quick to give
and still go slow enough
to bend to our faults, love comes
out of the shadows, unapologetic.

And one day, it cracks us open;
strips away our excuses, and exposes
our mesmerized hearts to the world.

Open Space

If an open space
begs to be filled
or held in the heart,
then this is a libation.

The old Gods still listen,
even though their ears
are weary of chatter.

They have had enough
of our neglect and would
rather let us drown

in our own hubris
than answer the prayers
hidden in our heart.

But they still love poetry
and will give a silent blessing
to one with a cup of verse.

This poem may not match
the metered beat of memory,
may lack the punch in a pack

of rhyming lines, but, if
it is held in the heart,
it can inspire angels

to spread their wings and
get the old Gods to open
the garden doors in welcome.

Don't Fret

Don't fret over the blank page.
The universe is filled
mostly with emptiness.

Isn't that enough to tell you
God loves nothing.

Isn't that what we yearn for?

The open field,
the empty calendar,
the duty-free day.

Savor the white space.
Let it be a sieve through which
your words fall into the void.

Let it stare you down
until it becomes a mirror in which
you no longer see yourself,
but, knowing you are there,
become all that is.

Step Out

We gathered raindrops
from the mouths of poets,
each a salve for the wrinkled soul,

intent to elevate pen to page,

as if we could, from the ashes of our lives,
ignite a fire as bright as the great mystics,

as if we could walk in their footprints,
left in the sand, before the grieving ocean
washes them away, and leaves us standing,

the sea swirling around our feet,
stealing our youth and vigor and we fall
into the weeping arms of God,

loving what we
cannot yet conceive,
yearning for what we
do not yet know how to do:

to step out into the country
that only exists outside
of all we have known and loved.

Be Ready

I keep my secrets here,
the ones I dare not
speak out loud,
that hide inside
the shy heart
and shameful soul,
not as a matter
of suppression
or to bolster
a weak ego
but as a shelter
for the pregnancy
of emerging powers.

Bless the irritant,
wrap it in love,
and it becomes a pearl.
Take the hardest
things in life and
cut them into diamonds.

Remember, even
the natural born hero
needs a catalyst
to don the cape.

So, when the water
breaks, be ready
for a miracle
in your life.

One Thing

If I loved only one thing,
it wouldn't be the blue sky,
not without clouds at least:
white, puffy mountains
shape-shifting in the drift;

it wouldn't be a Maple tree,
not without birds singing
from the branches at least
or raindrops sliding down
the leaves to make their own point;

it wouldn't be a summer day
on a mountain meadow,
not without dandelions at least
and wishes to blow to the wind;

it wouldn't even be this pen,
packed with poems, ink distilled
from the blood of gods,
not without a hungry page at least
to eat my words and your eyes
to drink them.

Loving one thing is never enough
for my spacious heart.

But oh how I love the pure silence
of this mountain meadow under an endless
blue sky that reaches beyond all wishes
while the ink of the unwritten in your eyes
is still fresh on the page.

Blanket of Quiet

Sometimes,
the soul asks a question
we cannot answer
except by being quiet.

And we do not know
if it will take a day,
a week, a year…

because the question itself
is often hidden from us.

But it calls us to nature,
to solitude, to the quiet
where we know all answers
are our own.

Then, one day, wrapped
in that blanket of quiet
like a cocoon, we emerge,

and we say to each other,
"I love what you love,"
without losing ourselves.

This is what the Buddha meant
when he spoke of compassion.

Labor Of Love

Peace is not a citadel
in the city of reason
or a pleasure palace
in the realm of the gods.

It is too easy to fall prey
to the allure of a steady state,
which is often the kiss of death.

Happily ever after is only
a feel good story ending,
ask any one who has been there
and they will tell you,

"All creation is a great
bursting forth out of stillness."

Breathing in the quiet
is a bath for the spirit
at the eye of the storm.

Cleanse yourself daily.
Then work in the field
of your creation.

That is the greatest
labor of love.

These Pools Of Light

These pools of light
into which I peer
blind me because
I cannot conceive of God
and all the names given
fall short of what
moves through me.

I tend to this world daily
but rarely do I sing to the stars
because I cannot conceive
how these tiny acts
manifest the divine.

My life weds
the secular and the sacred,
so why do I feel I must choose
one partner for the dance?

Do I not have two hands?
Two feet? Two eyes?

And this one inexplicable life,
however undeserved,
Calling out for my devotion.

I can only work myself
into a spirit worthy of love,
knowing I will still awaken
in a suffering world.

I refuse to turn my lips sour
even though I fear I will be
plucked from the vine and crushed
with the multitude into wine.

But isn't this how God distills us
into pools of light? Come,
let us drink our lives in,
and drunken, find god
in each other.

Prayers and Blessings

Prayer has always baffled and intrigued me. Since I was not raised with any religious orientation, I did not receive instruction in prayer. I understood it as an appeal to God or some divine presence, usually a request for blessing, protection, health, or good fortune for oneself or others. But I was never sure of the mechanics or the inner attitude one should adopt while praying. Despite my misgivings, I have a prayer practice. It sometimes seems made up or as if I am talking to myself, which at least is a way of setting intention, of aligning myself inwardly, and of sending goodwill out into the universe. I sometimes address my prayers to "the creator," or to the strnge angel I have always felt hovering around me. Some prayers have clearly come true. But, in most cases, I either do not know it manifested or it clearly did not manifest and this sense of disappointment is expressed in some poems in theis section.

I am more familiar, and more comfortable, with blessings. To bless is to affirm something deeply. The word comes from the latin root meaning to praise or to worship. To me, it is a fully congruent "yes" that comes from the heart. My personal mission is to bless and be blessed because I want to create a world in which we see and bring out the best in each other. This section includes poems that serve as prayers or as blessings or about such acts and how they may help us to live well.

Cathedral Of Silence

I let the silence
of the world
enter me:

spacious, beatific,
like an empty cathedral,
lit by ten thousand candles,
that holds the memory
of every answered prayer
throughout time;

a silence that cleanses you
of all trifles and small pleas
you might place before God

because God will only accept
the prayers that serve
your thriving and free
the world to be itself.

In this silence, there is
no asking and no receiving.

All prayers of the heart
are answered the moment
they become the living truth
of your life.

Shroud

Sunlight streams
through the eastern window
and lays a holy shroud
on the dining table.

But there are no faces
on it. Not yet.

At this late stage,
a stranger's love
means everything
to me. It's all
a question of
where to start.

With dedicated effort, I can
quell the tension at the base.
I can remove the boards
that blocked the door.
I can stop hiding
from the bogeyman.

Now, the ringing in my ears
makes me wonder:
"who is calling?"

There is no spy cam
to peek at the other side.
I have to answer it
before the face will appear

This is how I am learning
to pray to a living God.

Guest Of Honor

I want a poem to spring from my lips. Fully formed.
Words that pierce your heart with truth and beauty.
A light that guides your aimless spirit home.

An answer to the prayer you have kept secret,
hidden even from yourself, because it is
too precious to speak.

Here it is, sent to you in certified mail,
hermetically sealed, stamped and validated
as a gift from the gods, offering you
an invitation to your life,

to a gathering of all those who have loved you
in this world and the next;

to hear the appointed one speak
the unspeakable longing in your heart,
giving voice to your lifelong struggle
against yourself, when all you ever
really wanted was to be blessed

by a parent's pride in you,
a lover's desire for you,
a friend's trust in you;

and all you ever really needed was to open
your undisclosed heart to itself to hear
this poem spring from my lips fully formed,
celebrating you as the guest of honor
in this one precious life you are given.

True Nature

If tapping keys could spread the word or
transfer a cut of cloth from one mind to another;
and if we made the cut in our likeness
and served it with kindness, would we gather
as one and break bread together?

If a new Buddha touched his fingers to the earth,
would it spark a collective awakening?
Would the money changers then
leave the temple of their own accord
in that global change of heart?

If we knew the Earth was our mother
and our medicine, would we stop
choking the air and polluting the water
and let ourselves be healed?

What is the use of faith
if our feet stay on the beaten path,
if we cannot bring the left hand
and the right hand together in prayer?

If we can map the universe unfolding,
why is it so hard to look each other
in the eye and say, "You are a miracle."

We are all cut from that cloth;
but, having been cut, we lose sight
of our own true nature.

No Defense

The fool in me lives
on the edge of falling
and easily becomes
the shape of all things
in the landscape of love.

With this gift of entering,
of shapeshifting into the world,
I feel the preciousness
of our struggle to be human
as we divine our way
through our lives.

How many times must I die
and be born before I embrace
my own nakedness?

That I have no defense against life,
that I cannot stop the tidal wave
from drowning us all
or prevent my wingless
heart from flying to you.

If I could trace it all
back to the source,
before the first birth,
or find my way beyond
the last death, would I then
disappear from the mirror?

Or would the mirror disappear
and reveal the strange angel
who has loved me through it all?

Empty Words

I prayed to the air, empty words from
my Godless mouth to an earless God
because I refused to give a name
to one who inspired flood and fire
in the "holy" heart of those who kill

in that name. To me, you remained
A ghost, a backstory to keep the faith
in dark times while my lonely heart
riled against your supreme injustice.
If the world bends to your will,

your will is bent into righteous anger
spilling the blood of the innocent
on the temple floors. Shouldn't I
then be god-fearing, too, because
I am at the mercy of a tyrant

with absolute power who rules
by fear and fury, shouting out,
"empty shelves in your pantry
justify jihadi violence." So, I prayed
to the air on those empty shelves

as if, by this magic, I could fill
the pantry with love. But how
can I ever succeed when I speak
empty words with a godless tongue
into an earless god? Who then

can save us from ourselves?

Command Joy

The wriggling heat
may feel oppressed,
but if you keep
a giggle-happy thought
up an invisible sleeve,
you will command joy.

So let your muscles melt
into a sea-sway hammock,
let your mind waffle-up
with the heat-waves as if
offering a prayer of solace
to an angry god.

Let your heart
befriend beauty
and you will
line your pockets
with gold!

At the end of the day,
toss the leftovers
into your dreams
to become a canopy
of twinkling stars
serving as your guides
and protectors
through the night.

Wordless Prayer

I once prayed wordless
slapping back the joy
because I believed prayer
should be solemn.

But the years
have found a home
to ground my floating life.

Now, I look back
across a faultless desert
where I once believed
I was forsaken.

I once believed
meaning was found
in denial and that
it was my right
only to pursue
happiness, not
to have it.

On this matter,
I cheated the gods
serving smiles
more times
than I can count
while flying
under the radar.

I turned the tables:
I once stopped my life
to let the clock run.
Now, I stop the clock
to let my life run.

In this pause,
I find my oasis
and laughter runs
through me
like a wordless prayer.

Forked Tongue

Now that I have stepped out
of the river that was my life

and night has soaked me
through to the bone;

now that I am twice born and
can speak the language of trees,

I see my people in all the faces
hidden in the jungle, watching

over me from the invisible world
that goes with me wherever I go.

If I had known this 300 moons ago,
I would never have become a shoplifter.

Now, my closets, cluttered with things
that don't belong to me, teach me

a second language. But when I trace
my forked tongue back to its origins,

I speak of nothing but God to the invisible world
that goes with me wherever I go.

That's why the night can never have me,
even when it has soaked me to the bone.

That's why I sleep in a bed of gratitude
and wake up smiling.

The Archer And The Target

Think simple but not shallow,
like a lake that is so deep,
no one has seen the bottom.

You can rest your mind
on the smooth surface
and the depths will hold
all that is within you.

Through practice, you need less and less
until everything comes to the surface
and you disappear in the reflection.

That is how the Buddha
became light enough
to sit on a lotus flower.

But if you aim for a target;
enlightenment, or power, or peace of mind;
he will tell you to go be an archer because
the whole point of sitting is the practice
but the practice of sitting is pointless.

That is why you must cross your legs,
curl your fingers together, sit upright,
and concentrate on breath.

It's all just to give you something
to do, and to give the archer a target
in the practice, until you have
the strength to be the target.

Explaining Birth

I know the basic biology: how
sperm meets egg, merge, and then
the explosion of cellular division, duplication,
specialization mapping out a baby,

and a being with bone and blood and
brains, with heart and soul; pops out
of the birth canal nine months later.
But years later, when the child asked me

"why are we are born?" I am tongue-tied.
I invoke the gods and yammer about miracles.
It's one of those topics the conspiracy theorists
can spin all kinds of elaborate plots by aliens

or the prophets can weave into religion.
But I am not cut from that cloth. Unfortunately
I am neither a holy man nor a scientist.
So, when the child asks, I just say,

"let's go out tonight
and look for falling stars
so you can see
where you came from."

Holy Beholding

I want to be among those
who see what is possible beyond
the realms of magic and science,
whose eyes are lit by the sun
and whose fears and desires
have been cleansed in that flame.

They are unburdened spirits,
the breed of angels who peer back
at you, through the veil of time,
with a holy beholding.

They ask nothing of you
and need nothing from you.

They love you even though,
and actually because,
they know everything about you.

They are not yet consummated in spirit,
not yet blinded by the light and enrapt
in a love that is greater than this world.

They still see the separateness of beings
and they look at us with grieving hearts
because we are meant to fly and they
see us picking the wings off of each other.

Once among us, born of violence,
they know cruelty breeds cruelty
but they do not turn away, staying
steady on the liminal edge to lift
the veil that burdens your spirit
and look at you with a holy beholding.

Hiding Place

The world has too much to offer.
The day, with its relentless light,
eventually puts us all to shame.

A good hiding place is priceless.

You might find it in the temples
or retreat centers or the wild places
where only the fit and foolish go;

but only if you leave your "self" behind.

That's the trick. The real question is:
how do you hide from your self?
Who, you might ask, is speaking?

I speak as the one you don't see

in the mirror, the one looking back,
from behind your reflected eyes,
faceless, nameless, completely forgotten,

and forever with you.

Rude Awakening

This is my life in retreat,
on the inward shore of all things,
here to preach the gospel
of rude awakening:

that the empty cup
we hold out to life
like a beggar
is the holy grail.

When we look
to the world to fill us,
we forget that
it is our emptiness

that holds it all.
I lay a blanket on the sand,
a picnic table for us
to feast on the stars,

while bombs drop out there
in the shadowland of those
fighting for a fair share of coin.
They will say we are crazy,

when they find us, singing
our drunken songs; they will say
that our poetry is useless,
that we can't live on air.

But we say, "you can't
live without it," even as they
drag us back into the battle
and try to get us to trade

our cups for guns by telling us
it is for country, kin, and freedom.
But what is it worth to us when we
have nothing in which to hold it?

Raspberry Crush

If I sat down for a heart-to-heart with God,
I would ask where is the blue in the sky?

It may seem a silly thing to ask
when you have an audience with the Almighty.

But I have tried to sweep my hand
through the air to catch the color of that spirit.

It only took a single breath for her to give us light.
So, color is God's love poem for us.

It is both in the world and in the eyes that see it,
like the raspberry crush I felt for you the moment I saw you.

I can't tell you how many rosy dreams
followed that chance encounter.

I now know that moment was a time
that I had an audience with God.

But I was speechless, flooded with purple passion,
drinking in the honey yellow light of the moon

and I knew I would follow that raspberry crush
through the night. Now, only the color remains,

like so many cherished memories,
after the moment is gone.

In my next audience with God,
I will lay out all the colors I've lived

as if they are my love poem to life and,
if I am lucky, God will let out a raspberry crush sigh.

The Gospel of Radiance

Heaven & Earth

"Heaven" is one word that I was never shy about using in my poetry. It is common enough in everyday vernacular as a reference to any place that has the look and feel of paradise. So it was easy to rely on it as a placeholder for all our dreams of utopian freedom. Western spiritual traditions tend to place heaven faraway and beyond this life, as a reward for the righteous and its opposite, hell, as a punishment for the wicked, or for those infidels and unfortunate ones who lack faith or were not chosen. Earthly life certainly can be painful and depressing, not only at the hands of nature at times, but also, and perhaps more alarming, at our own hands given the brutality and inhumanity in our own treatment of each other. If we did not have some sense that good would be rewarded in this life or the afterlife (if there is one) then there might not be much impetus to be kind to strangers or help each other out in life. This set of poems is about the contrast between the magical paradise we long to inhabit and the brutal, but beautiful, world in which we live.

If Heaven Is Elsewhere

If heaven is elsewhere,
faraway and out of reach
in this lifetime, then let me
slip off these gravity boots
and find my joy in
the lightness of being.

I don't need to book a room
at the Shangri-La to let
my heart dance with the moon
or go see the last wild lions
in the Serengeti to dip
my heart into wild beauty.

If distance is metered
in the mind, then heaven
can always be found
in the nearness of the heart.

Never Give Up

I refuse to join the masses
who live a hard labor life
rather than be an easy target
and who tunnel out of the prison
of mediocrity with a spoon
rather than stand naked in the light.

I have had enough of darkened eyes,
stalking the light on moonless nights
when the clouds hide my destiny;

enough of the rudderless life
drifting in the wind hoping I might,
one day, hear the voice of God;

enough mining glory
from the trivia of my days
and seeking answers
in a book of dog-eared pages
to questions I've long forgotten.

But I won't be shedding tears

because I will never give up
on the power of an acorn
to produce an oak
or the drive of the salmon
leaping against the odds
to return to its source.

Spiritual Retreat

If you want to talk with God,
be prepared to have the roof
blown off of your life.

You've layered all your tissue paper
excuses into the thickness of castle walls,
but you secretly know they will not
withstand the siege.

You could make it quick,
climb to the top of the volcano,
and jump. But it's easier
to just call it quits.

Plan a trip to the desert
when the weather allows
and the skies are clear enough
to see the stars.

You can get there by car,
stay in a nice hotel,
enjoy the full spa treatment,
and call it a spiritual retreat.

Who made up the rule
that only hardship or disaster
can clear the wax from your ears?

Wouldn't God want you
to pamper your self?

Meanwhile, the crew back at home
is busy patching up the roof and walls
so that, when you return, you can forget
the catastrophe and go on with your life.

This Living

This living may be a bitter revenge
from the gods, laughing at our folly.
Our mistakes, our misgivings,
our hardships may be trivial
in a universe born of violence,

but we can still celebrate heroism
in the face of our suffering,
and find our own sweet revenge
in the delight we take in little things.

And then, we turn the tables,
laughing at ourselves, and
the gods are surprised to find
we are sitting beside them.

Let's Just Say

Let's just say, despite all the busy-ness,
that you arrive as if you are truly on holiday.

Let's just imagine everything in your life
is "taken care of" and that you left behind
the cluttered list and relentless demands.

In fact. let's say your whole life is actually a holiday.

You get this break in eternity to feel
the force of breath and beating heart,
to feel the biting chill of winter
and stinging heat of summer; you get
to shudder in the storms of nature
and to feel stuck in the boredom of routines;
you get fights over trivia, laughter with friends,
and hidden intimacies only a loving God could imagine.

This would account for why time speeds up
when you age because you know
the ride is nearing the end.

It's what you came for and if you want
to make complaint a part of the ride, then go for it.

You get it all, as much as you want.

Why not take if all? The only thing stopping you
is that you've already forgotten that you waited
in line for an eternity just for this short,
thrilling Disney ride of life.

If I Could

If I could tell you
the nine secrets of the heart,
guide you to the light,
give you a cup of the holy water,
forgive you and bless you,
and walk with you as
the companion of your life,

I would be steadfast in my love,
even when you shun me,
or when you look back
and see the wet footprints
we left in the sand washed away
by the tidal presence of life.

I would whisper the words
unspoken in your heart
to calm the raging sea
and clear the stormy clouds,
not as an escape from suffering
but as a reminder that you
are made of joy.

And I would lift you
out of darkness
and celebrate you in light
with unwavering faith
in your capacity to embrace
the whole of your life.

Ourselves

We remain ourselves
though we do not know
what we contain.
Our bodies are made
over and over again
with anonymous atoms.

We are bearers of stardust
and elephant dung.

Ancient winds blow through us—
whispers we can feel in our bones
and almost know in those nights
we are beyond sleep
when stillness lets us feel
a million unseen particles
leaping out into oblivion.

This truth slumbers
throughout our lives.
Yet, it is everywhere
around us, in us,
passing through us.

We give ourselves
to the universe
to be made new,
over and over again,
and we never know it
because we remain
ourselves.

The Call

If I took my chances,
I would make the call,
right out of the blue,
for no good reason,
on a whim, and joyfully.

I guess you could say
I would be indulging God.
I don't think he will pick up.
If I got the story straight,
it's his day of rest and
I believe it because…
Well, just look at things.

The day of rest has lasted
6,000 years. So, as you
can imagine, there is
a bit of a backlog.

Infinite Possibilities

I'm blowing the top of the intention game.
Out of infinite possibilities, I always choose
the ones nearest to me. I can blame it on
lack of imagination or poor magic, but it's
a lot less risky if you keep the target close.

The dreamer holds up the golden chalice and says,
"you're a hair breadth away from wonder."

The critic laughs, points out that
"you are no more than a stick in the mud."

But I can take it. I say the stick is
the stalk of the lotus and I will, one day,
blossom into a seat cushion for the Buddha.

For years, Buddha repeated,
"Each tiny awakening expands
the range of choosing until
the whole edifice cracks and
you become the chosen one."

He scoffs at my argument that I would rather
be the choosing one then the chosen one.

But in my heart, I know he's right:
it's just that I am deathly afraid
that I will actually be picked.

Live The Mystery

Today, I live the mystery of myself.
I walk in reverence, spirit bowing,
asking what ever God may exist
to shed me of my misled thoughts
and mistaken identity and
restore my animal presence.

The prayer, to live, is simple
enough, but the path is often
steep, storied with misgivings,
and littered with challenges,
both great and small, like those
that so often come dressed
in the everyday, stealing my
attention, distracting me from
the path and leading me astray.

I chant my mantra: "live on
the earth, be among the legged
and land-bound. Bring your levity
to the world, laughing at gravity,
standing up for yourself with
your feet firmly planted
on holy ground."

Another Tongue

When the hand is guided by the heart,
the pen becomes another tongue
that speaks of truth and longing,
the fire from the rim of what's
burning within you. It speaks

of twists and turns and broken promises,
of water lifted from the deep well
slipping through your fingers
back to the ground you stand on.

When pressed for your authority, be like
Buddha and touch your fingers to the earth:

"The only real sorrow is separation.
The only real blessing is beauty."

Follow the unenlightened
and you will live caged in a zoo.
So, heed your heart and
throw open all the locks.

Walk out of your cage as if
you no longer belong there
while everybody else is running
in the other direction.

It is not an act of courage
or stupidity, but of necessity.

Pray you will be ripped apart
by hungry alligators or mauled
to death by angry hyenas.

The liberated blood that appears

on the page is the ink of your truth
and your longing and it will,
at last, set you free.

Firefly In A Jar

When the thieves of time
sit at your death bed,

your heart saddened by what
they have stolen,

and they offer
what little light remains,
a firefly in a jar,

as a lantern
for your passage,

only a fool would refuse.

If you are willing to welcome
even the starless night,

if you have worked
your own heart into a garden,

you will accept, bowing
all the way down in gratitude,

kissing the earth farewell,
opening the jar with no regret,

and letting the light go free.

Hazing

Epilogue: for everything there is a season… from Ecclesiastes III

A hanging haze
drifts down the valley,
leaving a trail of tears
for those whose eyes
peer into the light.

We were not equipped
to live on fire.
We were born of water.

We traded fins and gills
for feet and lungs
and life on the land,

giving up that liquid embrace
for the thin air of promise.

We wanted the middle world,
between sea and sky,
so that we could have it all.

We wanted to be gods,
to claim the land,
to mine the world
of its treasures
while free of its duties.

And the gods gave us fire.
Now, we burn up the world
with our own divine spark.

The Life You Saved

In nineteen hundred and sixty nine,
the war was raging in your mind,
but you'll thank God for the March of Dimes,
to save your life a second time.

Even though you wallowed in the grass,
and blew your mind on the acid pass,
you looked death right in the eye,
and said "This time I'll pass you by."

At sixteen, you would never bend
until you "lost your head" giving in
at the whipping post when you let Dad win.

The March of Dimes could not save you then
but I'll tell you this, as a friend,
what you gave up in the end
you will spend years trying to find again.

The wild horse must first be tamed
to ride it across the wild plains.
And when the dream of unfenced land
is no longer enough to take a stand,

the wild horse becomes a man
who tries his best to understand
what's left to do with his own hand.

At sixteen, it's hard to know,
that freedom is only half of the show
among the questions you had to ask:

Who is riding on my back?
Whose in charge of my heartstrings?
What makes me do all these things?

The Gospel of Radiance

In nineteen hundred and sixty nine,
there were no answers you could find
but I can tell you this, my friend,
it all worked out in the end.

You'll rip the posters from your wall.
You'll drop off the psychedelic call.
And I'm here to thank you from the heart
when you took the chance at that fresh start

because you turned yourself on a dime
and the life you saved at that time
was not just yours, but also mine.

Waiting For A Ride

There is a longing in me
to slow down these wild horses
and feel the ground beneath my feet,

to take a stand for what I love
in the face of enemies,

to brew a cup of wonder and
share it with everyone I meet;

to toss away these empty dreams
and open up my life,

to drop the beggar's cup
and reach for the light;

and to hold my hand out
to those who suffer
through the night

because there is a longing in me
to get it all just right

but I know it will never be enough:

I'm just a man with a broken heart
at the Buddha bus stop
waiting for a ride to Paradise.

The Gospel of Radiance

Gods & Guides

The poems in this section refer to specific religious icons or mythic characters. I had particularly strong reservations when such figures appeared in my poetry. I want my poems to be easily accessible and such references seemed to require explanation, especially since religious icons and mythic stories are already laden with connotations that I may not know, or that I may be using differently. Some people may find my use of such references upsetting, insulting, or even blasphemous. Unfortunately, religious ideologies have inspired some of the worst conflicts on the planet. I do not like conflict and I do not wish to create it. This is one reason I was hesitant to publish this book.

Despite my effort to distance myself from religion, I have a very strong sense of the beloved as a spiritual presence in my life and most of my poetry is inspired by or written to the presence of the beloved. I call this presence the *Secret Sharer*, a name I borrowed from the Joseph Conrad short story, which made a deep and lasting impression on me when I first read it as a teenager. In Conrad's story, the newly appointed captain of a ship harbors a fugitive from justice in his cabin and ferries him to safety risking the ship and crew to set him free. Conrad's Secret Sharer is a shadow self that lives a moral code of his own and that inspires the captain to claim his authority in life.

My Secret Sharer has played a similar role, although, in my case, it has taken 40 years to ferry this daemon to safety. Mine differs from Conrad's in that she is not so much a harbinger of authority as an invitation to love. I loved the name Secret Sharer because I have always felt that the door to a profound intimacy may open at any moment with any person, and, in fact, happens all the time outside of our awareness. The clerk in the store may be your coach, the driver of the taxi may be your teacher, the lady in the line may be your lover, and the stranger on the street may be your savior. The real story of our lives is in this subtext of the soul, where we are in constant conversation with each other. This soul friend is the one thread that ties my life together, that anchors me to my heart, and that urges me on toward a light I cannot see.

The Secret Sharer

The secret sharer
is the angel
in whose arms
I have lived my life,
the presence that walks
with me in shadow and light,
who never tires of me no matter
how much I rant or how far afield I stray,
who is always eager to call out the essence
of me and ever ready to catch me when I fall.
The secret sharer is the one whose boundless love
blesses all the magic and all the mess of my life.

A "Pinch Me" Moment

This is the river that nourishes me,
my heart awash with joy, the songs of my life
remembering me back and a moon rising
as if it is a clarion call to love something
everywhere nameless.

If this is a "pinch me moment,"
let me be a pin cushion because
my skin is tingling to your hidden voice.

You never told me that your love is freedom,
that I could ride that current into Grace,
that there is a radiance even the darkness loves.

I'm standing at the altar like a man who
orchestrates events to surprise himself
and then, is surprised when he does.

Laughing, you add, "And you play
that game again and again!"

"No," I tell you, "in this case,
I am the baby Moses in a basket
before becoming your mouthpiece."

So Go ahead —
toss me in the river.

Jesus In A Hot Air Balloon

I saw Jesus in a hot air balloon.
He said, "don't put all your eggs
in one basket" and then joked,
"that is the reason for the holy Trinity."

I noticed the ropes were straining to hold
the balloon down against the thrust of ascension
as he began a sermon proclaiming he returned
to clean the windows on the skyscraper of truth
and to preach "a new gospel of radiance."

But the ropes could no longer hold,
and, unraveling, his voice disappeared
as it lifted into the sky. He continued
speaking as if this was to be expected.

Someone in the crowd yelled, "He is risen!"

We hopped into a caravan of cars to chase
the rainbow colored balloon across the sky.

Eventually, it went where roads could not go,
drifting over the hill, and disappearing.

Someone leaned over to me and asked,
"do you believe?" He showed me his cell phone
and all the pictures were a blur of colors.

Then, like a wave of wonder sweeping through
the crowd, everyone looked at their phones,
checking photos, the colors blurred, and the video
was light streaks with the sound of whistling wind.

The Man In The Moon

Epigraph: Begin with the end in mind. —Stephen Covey

When the fingers of his right hand
lifted in blessing and those of the left
offered the sacred heart, I bathed
in the light, becoming a reflection,
and, like the waning crescent moon,
bowed for days until I disappeared
into his embrace. This is how I turned
my face away from earthly things.

"Who, then, lives in your home?" you ask.
"You mean the one who picks up the mail
addressed to 'occupant?'" I query back
and then add, "I barely know the man."

The truth is, he is a fugitive from the law,
even though he never committed
the crime for which he feels guilty.
So, he had to erase his name
and live in the shadows.

"Will you take his place?" "No," I tell you,
"I will lift my fingers in blessing
and offer my sacred heart to him."
I will call him the man in the moon,
because he always unknowingly
faces his source, even when
he grows dark and seamless
while grazing in heaven.

One day, no matter how many moons it takes,
I know he will see me and turn himself in.

Buddha Came To Visit, Uninvited

There was no question
of his belonging in my house,
stretched out on the sofa,
head propped up on his left hand,
looking at me as if I were the guest
in my own house and not he.

"You've waited your whole life,"
he said, "for someone to say to you:
come home."

I wept.

I wanted to wash his feet.
He refused, laughing,
and said, "that is another faith."

He instructed me,
articulating every word,
as if this was the whole of his teaching:

"Wash your own feet as you would mine."

I did not want to take off my shoes,
ashamed of the hole in my sock.

But he spared me my embarrassment,
changing the subject, wanting to hear
the latest gossip. It was only then
that I realized how much
he loved this world.

The Hungry Ghosts

Mother Mary ascended into heaven
on this day, but we have lost our way.
Even though the earth is tilted and
we have dug ourselves into a hole
with our lust and our greed,
all is well in the scheme of things.

Tragic though it may be
whenever sentience suffers
or the flame of life is extinguished,
the great beyond ultimately has
no need for us despite our hubris.

It is, in fact, just the opposite.
We are nothing without the cradle of life
to give us breath and replenish our blood.

I pray for human kindness, but
when I listen to the hungry ghosts
that walk among us, I know
prayer alone will not save us.

Jealous God

You have to find a quiet hiding place, lean in,
and whisper in the hushed voice of those who
share secrets when you pray to a jealous god.

It is easier than you think, even in the crowded
hallways, because any corner of the mind will do.

You do not need to bend a knee or bow
your head in the humble way of the supplicant.

Your words do not need a gracious spring,
do not need to ride the outward flow
of the heart, do not need to be an offering
of light in a dark world. No. Your jealous god

can still be merciful. You do not need to
cast aspersions upon the favored or
delight when they fall because such
sentiments are only icing on the cake.

You can play your cards close to the chest,
conducting silent inquiry, asking why they get
what you don't, as you walk the path
to the temple doors. Or better still, simply

designate the target and let the god shoot arrows,
while you, smug in your spiritual heaven,
can still walk with your head held high.

Salt Pillar

He said he was guided by some unspoken voice
to take us and flee from iniquity, never looking back.

I fell behind. I could hear the pack closing in.
At first I thought it was a growling sound,
then heard it as the cooing of doves.
At first I thought it was teeth nipping at my feet,
then felt it as a soft tongue licking my ankles.

I could not tell if this love was angel,
human, or animal, but the unyielding desire,
the want of me, rose from the ground,
from the banished land, from the place
I was taught where sin takes root in the heart.

But it was so gentle, so joyous, so happy
to breath its prayer on my skin, as if
I was the answer. I stopped.

I turned into that yearning embrace
as the desert liquified, rose up, swelling
all around me, flushing my thighs with tiny kisses,
like sea foam bubbles popping with ticklish delight,
rushing into me, lifting and thrusting, the earth
quaking in my hips, until the word dislodged.
exploding from my belly, blowing off the lid,
erupting up my spine and a flock of doves
flew out of my gaping mouth singing praise
to a different God than the one above.

I left with that sea as it drained out,
never looking back, not even wanting
to look back, but leaving behind a salt pillar
that those with desert eyes use as a warning.

Angels

I

It is recorded
in the Registry of Heaven
for everyone to read:
one hundred thousand angels
came and camped outside your birthplace.
They waited for you to come into the world,
forming concentric circles, heads bowed
and white feathered wings fanning out
into a mandala—an eye of which
you were the iris

II

It is written
in the Book of Days
for everyone to read:
one hundred thousand angels
follow you daily as your life spans
the arc of a covenant from midday to midnight,
from dawn to dusk, forming the cardinal points
of a compass and an arrow line of winged light
which always points to your own true north.

III

It is ordained
by the Law of Destiny
for everyone to read:
one hundred thousand angels
will testify in your defense on the day
of atonement; their brilliant wings
blurring into the white light
that will guide you
through the tunnel
and to the gates
of heaven.

Resurrection

If the Phoenix strays too far from the truth,
it will burn in its own fire.

That is how it skirts the edges of immortality,
rising from the ashes to become itself again.

Could this have been the same fire
that burned after the burial stone

rolled across the mouth of the tomb
where Jesus's body was laid to rest?

Buddha took a different path,
pledging his allegiance to the earth.

He knew the apple was tainted
When he ate it. But he never
left the garden, he just saw

that it had weeds too.

Mother Mary

Mornings are my niche.
A recess in the day and, today,
it is an altar of awakening,

On it the figure of Mother Mary,
her head bowed, turned slightly
to the right; her hand on her heart,
clutching a necklace.

I feel the piety of a thousand lifetimes
as a devotee. How else can I account
for the unyielding beauty of this
heart-broken life?

Everything about her says,
"the time is ripe."

I want to know what jeweled treasure
or sacred relic she holds
in her clenched hand, believing
it could be the answer.

I know what it isn't, although
I don't know how, saying:
"It is not a cross to bear,
or a flaming heart, or a locket
with the image of a shepherd.
Is it?" She says, "No, it is
a vial for the fallen,"
then she lifts her coy eyes,
looking directly at me, her
voice laden with innuendo:
"And it is empty."

Having A Beer With The Buddha

If only little awakenings were cumulative.
Perhaps then one day I will wake up
and look Buddha in the eyes.

We could go have a beer together,
laugh at all the years striving to be effortless
and the irony of seeking enlightenment
while hanging a "do not disturb" sign on my door.

I would ask him what one secret
we might plant in the heart of my next slumber.
I imagine us feeling giddy, planning the perfect prank.

I say, "Let's change the sign to "Open For Business!"
Laughing, Buddha says, "And add: Walk-Ins Welcome!"

Suddenly, a long-haired, bearded stranger,
who was eavesdropping on our conversation,
leans in, "Then, if you really want to get him,
we will…" he says circling his hand
as if to bind us in a conspiracy, "...dress up
as ICE agents and demand to see
his proof of citizenship."

Buddha and I are taken aback,
We look at him and exclaim, in unison,
"Jesus Christ!"

Echo

In the first light, when things are still
steeped in shadow, the rooftop skyline
appears as canyon ridges.

I hear the faint echo of your voice,
calling my name, as if you are trapped
somewhere in the ancient rocks

pleading for love. I know this moment:
it is déjà vu one thousand times over.
It has been this way ever since

I turned to stone. It was the only way
out of myself; the only way to make
room for my blossoms. Who can

still see the shape of me, kneeling,
or hear the prayer I silently say
to myself? I think "no one but you."

The "punishment" of the gods seems
cruel only in a world that demands
"happily ever after." The awakening

is fleeting, light comes crashing over
the edges, sweeping away the scene.
Your last words, an exclamation: "Look!"

In the distance I see a double rainbow.

The Master's Stick

Enlightenment, in the digitized mind,
is a switch, either on or off:
a koan solved, a whack
from the master's stick,
a single brushstroke
of calligraphy, water
on the pavement,
in the hands of a poet.

To expect it is to be like
a dog with Buddha nature
barking up the wrong tree.

The game is not there, no
matter how closely you look.

It may take a hundred
thousand sunrises before
the light that has, everyday,
struck your eyes to suddenly
touch your heart and you say
"Ahhh…"

"But," you ask,
"isn't that like
the masters stick?"

"Yes, and that was
the 100,000th whack."

Appointment

Unfurl yourself into the night.
Stretch to the stars.
Welcome the twinkling light
that has traveled across galaxies
to find your eyes in order
to give you this message:

"You are the completion
of all tomorrows,
the beginning
of all yesterdays,
the midwife
of all moments.
You are birthing
the living presence
into the world."

You may feel yourself
to be a tiny doorway,
but yours is the entryway
for the entire universe
to turn into life.

Fling it open.

Step out of yourself
and let the infinite
be your calling card

You have
an appointment
with God.

Conclusion

I am an agnostic because I do not know or cannot say with confidence that there is a god. I am also a believer that there is some greater intelligence operating in me, in the world around me, in the greater forces of life, and perhaps, as in Star Wars, woven throughout the fabric of the universe. Despite my unknowing, or unwillingness to make a claim about my spirituality, the poems in this collection arise out of a deep sense of the divine, a desire to make my life sacred, to live with reverence, and to find my place of belonging in the web of life. A core question in this search is: Where, or on what, do I center my life?

To me, the solution to the question about where to center myself is on the other within me, what you might call the "holy ghost" (which describes it perfectly to me, even though that term is so laden with Christian doctrine), or what I sometime call the Secret Sharer: that greater intelligence that includes my unconscious and beyond. I think of it like nested Russian dolls: the center is both inside of me and I am inside of the center of the greater self. The larger self contains me. The goal is to anchor my little "s" self in the core of the capital "S" Self.

I can't say exactly what this means or describe how to do it. Setting the intention is a great step. I also have numerous practices that serve this purpose to varying degrees and with relative success, including meditation, contemplation, specific guided processes I have invented for myself, self-hypnosis, and art. Writing poetry is, by far, the method that most aligns me with something greater than myself because the work often flows through me and is clearly co-created.

Compiling the poems for this book brought me face-to-face with a rather surprising issue and one that may seem strange given my agnosticism and my confused and conflicted relationship with spirituality. Many of the poems included in this set express a profound disappointment in God. My doubts have very deep roots, but, in a strange way, that disappointment is founded on a deeper underlying and undying belief. Disappointment requires expectation and my dismay at the silence of God, my lament over unanswered prayers, my unfulfilled longing for divine union, and my anger and confusion over the suffering of the good in a tyrannical world all rest on a bedrock of faith. If I had the chance and the courage, I would say to God, "You completely broke my heart. And yet here I am, at your feet again, to tell you it 's worth it because you also gave me poetry."

Why The Doubt?

If I could ride the rainbow
to the bucket of gold or
take the ten steps north
from the third tree near
the painted rock and feel
my shovel strike the buried chest,
or guess the winning number
in the lottery mega pot,
would I give up poetry?

If by stroke of misfortune,
I was rendered mute,
my body paralyzed,
unable to compose,
would I give up poetry?

My heart lives in that stream,
but would I still believe
after countless years of drought
and no manna from heaven in sight?

I have danced dangerously close
to that edge, even taken the leap
a few times, and each time,
I was saved by poetry.

So why the doubt?
My muse says, "fallen angels are
the only ones who argue with god
and that is exactly why god
loves them the most."

If that love is called poetry,
then I am a poet
and I have struck gold.

In closing, I offer a poem written after experiencing a dark night of the soul. I fell into nested loops of thought and, on several occasions, I lost the thread, and therefore the context for a line of thought. This brought up fears about losing my short term memory and how I could actually "lose my mind." I had a very palpable taste of dementia. But I also felt another part of me witnessing the whole thing despite all the looped thoughts and anxious feelings. I repeated a mantra, "I am here," as if spoken from the position of an unburdened witness and composed this poem:

I Am Here

The ancients painted the ceiling with stars
in the dark cave of the self, where they
played the music of bone and skin and
they danced their life into the ground.

They knew it was coming long before
ice fractured the world and splintered
the old ways into factions.

Then, the tribes lost the beauty of pure reflection.
They cursed their dissembled eyes and, from that
point forward, all mirrors were coated with shame.

When I lit a fire in that cave, the spirits
danced the worst atrocities of my fear and desire.

I was saved, standing on the ground
they made holy by their sacred vows
as they deputized me to speak the long
forgotten words that break the curse:

I am here to restore
the transparency of glass.

The Gospel of Radiance

Addendum

The Holy Man Letters

I have a practice of writing letters to my future self. I select a date on the calendar and then I write a letter in Evernote with a reminder to read it on the selected date. I have an agreement with myself not to read the letter until the set date. The one exception to this rule is a letter that I wrote on December 20, 2014 to be read on January 1, 2020. It was also the first time I imagined receiving a letter back and the first reference to me as a holy man. Included below are those two letters and a few additional notes written in the intervening years about the notion of being a holy man. I do not claim that I have achieved that status. To me, such a status is given to you, not something that you can claim. But I am clear that my inner self holds the possibility as a vision or direction to guide me in my becoming.

Marvel At This Life
Letter to 2020 Nick

I see you sipping champagne together with one who charms your heart and fills your eyes with beauty in one of those moments when you marvel at your life—a life beyond even your wildest dreams from my time five years ago. You may not feel me there, but I witness you indulging the world, unfurling your heart to the moment so that all other moments drop away. I watch you spread your soul out like a blanket of love amazed that you remain calm, somehow, even though the quiet joy in you is strong enough to power a universe. I marvel with you at this life even though I do not know your days or your desires. I have no need to know for I know your days are your own. You live in the temple of presence. You carry your bearing in life with you. You place your faith in the compass of your soul and you act in accordance with life.

I don't need to tell you that you have arrived, that this love has come to you because you have come to yourself and because you have embraced every particle of your life. I will tell you this: you are so much bigger now. The power you once sacrificed to your fears has been restored to you. Whatever held you back, the thing you thought you needed to be yourself, that kept you small and separate from all others, had to go. This is my one question of you: how did you do it? I want your guidance in this matter above all others because this is where our rivers merge.

I whisper my request in the breeze, tickling your skin, hoping that you will know it is me, that you will hear my plea and answer. You peer into the twilight as if you yourself are among the stars. You speak into your phone. I know you are writing to me, sending starlight back in time, sending soil from the future, sending the seeds of my destiny as if you are arranging a gift basket topped with champagne dreams sparkling with your wisdom. That little smile as you talk hints at the grand adventure that you know awaits me.

You know it is not the words that appear on the screen that will make the difference even when they show up in my heart clear as a bell on that one beautiful day that you so vividly remember and I have yet to live. It is the moment the echo of you becomes my voice, the moment the shadow of you becomes my substance, the moment when our rivers merge into the one God we serve. —Love from the one you once were.

The Dawn Draws Near

Reply from the 2020 Nick:

I give my heart in gratitude to you and with delight knowing the day draws close for our union. You have already spoken your truth. You have already mapped the lay lines of your soul. You have already written your vows. You already know what is required because you have written of it to me and heard of it from me many times. Now is the time when your word becomes your life.

The date is set. The place arranged. A surprise awaits. I will tell you this: I did not notice the importance of it at the moment but I have spent years living that surprise into life. The real magic comes from what unfolds after that because you begin to live as if every act is the act of a lifetime, as if each movement and every utterance is a declaration of your life. You go beyond being an advocate for love and become an embodiment of love.

This is your ascension, your elevation into to the calling of your youth, the calling you denied on the campus of Chabot College, the path you elected not to follow when you chose psychology over religious studies. You knew your light was not bright enough to withstand the world. You knew you needed to cocoon your love until you grew your wings. You crowned yourself the fool, the poet, the man of wisdom. Now you crown yourself with spirit. You came as an old soul and you knew this: to live according to the dictates of love is to turn your life over to God and to become a holy man.

I know there is still fight in you over this. I know you denied this path in part because you could not reconcile yourself with prescribed religious precepts and practices. And you knew the dangers of giving yourself over to God before you had a self to give. But you have been righting yourself with life. You have found the heaven in your heart. You have opened your eyes to an endless horizon. You have tuned your heart to divine whispering. You have begun to live the poetry of life.

You are now awakening to the universe, to the one power that turns all of creation. You have always known the key to the kingdom is love. But it is not a key you turn with your hands or with your heart. It is a key you turn with your life. Then, the doors open, God gives you His word, and....

What comes after can only be known by living the prayer of life. Meet me at the appointed hour as we have agreed. Our communion will be made manifest. Until then, practice your becoming. Live the prayer of life. —Love from The One Whom You Have Always Been

Facing The Trial

John O'Donoghue says, "To be holy is to be able to be inner and to be able to rest in the house of belonging…"

I look to you, the one who claims this destiny as a holy man, and ask how I qualify? What justifies such a pronouncement? Monday was Martin Luther King, Jr. day, a day to celebrate the reverend who forced us to look in the mirror as Americans, who changed the face of America by his dedication to peace and to stand firm in the face of injustice. He was a holy man.

I look to Gandhi who changed a nation by his own unwavering resolve in a greater good and in the ability of his people to rule themselves. I look to the great mystics, to Kahlil Gibran, to Rumi, to Hafez and say, "I am not the equal of holiness." Yes, I know that I, like all others, live by grace of the holy ghost, that my nature is divine, that I am sanctified by God simply by my presence, which is ordained by God. But to be a holy man among humanity, to be an advocate of the spirit is a calling that I fear is beyond me. I am no Martin Luther King, No Gandhi, no preacher from the pulpit. I have not lived a life devoted to ideals of social justice, I have not risked my life for love or for any cause. How can I call myself holy when I have lived so far short of holiness?

I know this protest will fall on deaf ears, that you have already claimed this space despite how unwarranted it may be, that you have already stepped into this presence. I do not begrudge you. I do not cast aspersions on you. I do wonder, however, how you live with yourself knowing what you know about how I have lived and what I done. How you can claim yourself to be greater than the life you have lived, more true to spirit than the life you have lived, more in touch with the truth than the life you have lived. This is my indictment, my charge, This is why I place you on the stand. Can you face the trial?

Another Lifetime

The last time I sat here was another lifetime. If I didn't keep all this gut-clenching, heart wrenching tension holding onto the tracks, I would slip away into this world. All the stories are true in the place of my belonging, so I am careful about which ones I live. In my telling, shadows slow dance with the light making love at my feet and the clock meters out another paycheck with every tick. Even road rage thistles the ground with spiked medicine when I brew it into a tea; my grief is the crowned dandelion upon which I blow my wish to heaven; and my sadness is the baptismal water from which I am reborn into my life; all the rest is celebration.

There really is nothing to hold on to and nothing to run away from. So, why the unyielding tension? It all comes down to a dead story I have carried with me through so many lifetimes: I've lived the premise that everything I say and do will be held against me in the court of life. They haven't found the body yet. But when they do, I better have an alibi and, in my recycled moments, backward beeping into yesterday's lifetime, I build my case, with gut-clenching, heart-wrenching tension, praying for acquittal. If I bury that story, I am reborn into this life. There is no charge against me, no trial to stand, no judge to sway, and no jury to win. They are only shadows making love at my feet as the clock ticks out another paycheck.

The Three Sacrifices

This was written in fulfillment of an assignment from the class, "A day of Creation with the Toltec Shaman Don Jose Ruiz," the son of Don Miguel Ruiz, author of the popular book T*he Four Agreements.* The assignment was to identify three things you are willing to let go in your life, invest each one in a stone and release them into nature. Below is a transcript of my dictated notes during the "ceremony:"

I'm taking this walk alongside the polluted water as my act of contrition while a duck, keeping pace with my step, swims, feeding in the algae-rich canal. I pass by patches of it, shimmering green and I stop long enough to see dendritic tentacles branching out as if it is an exposed brain. Up ahead is the bridge across the canal where I will drop my stones.

I wonder: How long has it been since I sat beneath a tree? I choose one with a perfect view of the bridge where I will make my three sacrifices. The rough bark bites my back and the hard ground doesn't give, doesn't form itself to my shape. For a moment, I wish I were at home, leaning back in a comfy recliner. The tree and the ground are not being resistant or defiant. It is the world saying, "take me as I am."

I do a dress rehearsal, imagining myself dropping the stones, one by one, into the dirty canal. First, letting go of "sex as an obsession." That one is easy since age has already taken off the edge and it has always been about union with the divine. Second, releasing "sensuality as sin" and embracing my body as a sacred temple. If I am ever to be holy man, I know it starts as caretaker of the temple. The only question that remains is: what replaces the third sacrifice when I drop the old belief that "my life is on trial."

I feel the motors working, as if I have to have an answer before I make the sacrifices. I sit with eyes closed for what seems an eternity and nothing comes while the wind furiously whips around me. I give it up, trusting something will emerge, and the wind suddenly stops.

Upon standing, I see an acorn, freshly fallen and still capped by the bark of its maker. I pick it up as my sign and walk toward the arch where I will perform my silent ceremony.

For each one, I say prayers of gratitude, for the gifts given and for the service those old beliefs have rendered to me. They have kept me from running afoul of the law, helped me build up a decent reputation, driven me to live a good life, and to stay within the lines even though I have stretched those lines to accommodate a unique life. They have taught me the constraints of the world and how to live within them, and they have given me the blessing of vigilance over myself. While I make my offerings, I'm aware of the world around me. I look from side to side to make sure no one is watching before I toss each of the stones over the edge. On the third stone, after catching myself looking both ways, I think, "this is my last apology" and I release the "trial life" to the water.

On the way back, pondering what new belief will take root, I realize that this act, like everything else is a shell, a seed, like the acorn I picked up, a holder for the unfolding of life. This is the closest thing I can get to a new belief: That I am the tree of life. I feel my roots are deepening, that I am, at last, suckling the mother, and that she is wholly delighted in giving me her nourishment. I suddenly realize, all this while, I have been in a state of exquisite attention, acting intentionally, with a profound feeling of kindness toward myself and I realize it is a simple and profound act of loving myself. What is love if not this kind of exquisite attention? When I strip away all the silly judgments and petty emotions, I am always there, on both sides, giver and receiver, lover and beloved. The core message from don Jose was to treat yourself and your life as if you and your life are "the love of your life." As a final act of the ceremony, I come to my "self" and say the words I gleaned from Don Jose: "I am here for you. I will protect you from any harm, I will give you any dream. I will serve you in every way even if it means, at times, saving you from yourself."

The Last Word

I cannot say I am any closer to being a "holy man" than I was several years ago when that phrase singed my ears. Perhaps the idea is just a distant star that twinkles in my eye and keeps me on a fool's errand in life. When it comes to the end, perhaps I will have a plot near Don Quixote or a win a placard for a Walter Mitty life. To tell you the truth, I always thought skeletons look like they are smiling as if they got a good laugh out of the utter absurdity of it all. Perhaps, in the end, I'll get a good laugh out of my audacity to argue with god believing I could get in the last word!

The Gospel of Radiance teaches me to take things lightly because reverence is ultimately joyful and holiness is profoundly playful. My things, actions, thoughts and feelings are not sacred in themselves. My life is not sacred in itself. All are made sacred by my relationship to them and the light, or the quality of exquisite attention, I shine on them. It is all so much simpler than my big brain wants to believe and my indomitable ego needs in order to feel special. Take, for example, this snippet from an argument with God:

Jesus said, "If those who lead you say to you, 'See, the kingdom is in the sky,' then the birds of the sky will precede you. If they say to you, 'It is in the sea,' then the fish will precede you. Rather, the kingdom is inside of you and it is outside of you. When you come to know yourselves, you become known, and you realize you are children of a living god. But if you will not know yourselves, you dwell in poverty and it is you who are that poverty."

--The Gospel of Thomas

Me: I wasn't expecting a handout, but I wanted more from you.

God: That's the whole problem. A handout is all I can give. It is called grace. And you refused it

Me: Then why all the talk about the chosen people or the require-
        ment of blind faith?

God: That is for goodness sake. And for you to learn to love your-
        self. If I give you a temple and you fill it with crap and neglect
        the upkeep, how can you appreciate the beauty of who you
        are?

Me: Why didn't you just say so?

God: I did, many times. You won't do it for yourself or even to save
        yourself. You don't think you are good enough. You need a
        greater purpose or a savior. So, I laid out a carrot and a stick.
        And you call me cruel? Claim I am showing favorites? You
        put yourself in the straight jacket.

Me: What about my prayers? My search for a sign. Why the silent
        treatment?

God: I answered every single one to the degree of your conviction.
        The faith I ask from you may not have any justification, may
        be completely unproven, but it is not a blind faith. It is unwa-
        vering faith in your own vision, in your own second sight.

Me: Isn't that just another way of saying I am not doing enough?
        That you are as disappointed in me as I am disappointed in
        you.

God: See, I am granting your wish in this as in everything else. I
        always let you have the last word.

Could this be true? My whole life has been a prayer answered, a
wish fulfilled? I always thought prayer was a deep desire, spoken
with intention and addressed to a greater power, not a living truth at
the heart of my life that gets fulfilled without ever being spoken. A
disappointment lived there, deep down under all the good I pro-
fessed, underneath all the love for which I longed, and that prayer

has been fulfilled. Now, I begin to live a new truth as a spirit in the world. At this point in my life, for my last words, I return to the first words God spoke in the Hebrew bible: "Let there be light" and I offer this Gospel of Radiance shining as brightly as I can.

The Gospel of Radiance

Notes

These notes are offered to give interested readers the background and inspiration for some of the poems in the collection and to cite the sources for the selected poems previously published:

From ***Heaven In Our Hearts*** (2012):
Down To The Bone
Ourselves

From **Divine Whispering** (2014)
This Is Poetry
Light
Lumbering Angels
Cathedral of Silence

From the **Work of Being Yourself** (2016)
Appointment

From **Bearing Witness** (2018)
Sieve
No Excuse for Light
These Pools of Light
Wordless Prayer

In The Shadow of Your Silence: I wrote this poem while steeped in the radical house purging method advocated by Marie Kondo in which you toss out anything that does not spark joy. (Pg. 19)

Radical Acceptance: Written in response to a writing prompt from the poet Mark Nepo to choose rather we would choose to be a door or a window and why. (Pg. 20)

The Gospel of Radiance: The poem served as the title piece for the book because it opened the floodgates to spiritual references in my poetry and inspired me to collect this set of poems. I had my doubts about the title both because of its boldness and potential repercussions and because I feared the content would not live up to the title. To be honest, I am still learning what the *Gospel of Radiance* might actually mean. This is normal for me because many poems arrive as preludes to something unfolding in me or in my life. (Pg. 1925)

When You Are A Stranger: As a frequent traveller, I often people watch. I enjoy imagining what it might be like to be someone else and this poem is about that experience. (Pg. 28)

Karmic Carousel: This frivolous poem actually is quite profound for me. Since poems often "come to me," I occasionally analyze them as if they are written by someone else, by referring to the "author" or "narrator." In this poem, the narrator raises the question of whether or not he loves god. He doesn't know and wagers a bet based on God's statement that "the elk loves the wolf before the kill," implying humans love god even when they are troubled or tortured. The narrator doubts this and bares his neck for God to take him as a wager. If he dies and does not love god, he wins and is off the karmic carousel. However, if he does love god, he asks to come back as a koala bear. (Pg. 30)

Dharma: This was written after a tour of the Aryan Bhumi Temple outside of Kuala Lumpur. This little temple was once the house of a wealthy Malaysian man. When he became ill, he donated the property to the local Rinpoche, who converted into a temple. The place definitely had a special feeling to it. (Pg. 35)

Native Tongue: I wrote this in July 2018 after hearing the poet Mark Nepo tell to the story of the original language all humans shared before God dissembled languages as a punishment for the Tower of

Babel. (Pg. 37)

Step Out: Written at a Writing Workshop with James Lee Jobe, the Poet Laureate of Davis, California. There were 6 of us present, including James and we each read two favorite poems by well known poets to each other and then used the tone, feel, imagery, and content from those poems for our own writing session. Many of the lines in this poem were stolen from what the other five poets read. (Pg. 43)

Shroud: Written one morning when the light streaming through the eastern window cast light and shadow on the dining table in a panel configuration that reminded me of the holy shroud with the alleged imprint of Jesus on it. (Pg. 53)

The Archer and The Target: I've read a bit about Buddhism, but I am not a practicing "buddhist." I do have practice of meditation, which is a mix of my techniques and some simple training in meditation I received along the way. This poem is about the challenge of "doing nothing," or just being, in mediation versus aiming for a target, which can include the tools used to focus attention while meditating. (Pg. 62)

Raspberry Crush: Written at Marie Writer's session on led by Ann Michaels, *Raspberry Crush* captures the playful nature of the divine. (Pg. 68)

Infinite Possibilities: We are driven, and often conflicted, by the twin drives of belonging (blending in or fitting in) and authenticity (being uniquely oneself). The desire to be picked or chosen can be perceived as a deep affirmation of both belonging and uniqueness: you are unique because you are chosen and, in being chosen, you belong especially loved by God. (Pg. 80)

Another Tongue: I wrote Another Tongue as an ode to free writing after a WeChat conversation with a student who praised the practice which she had incorporated into her life. (Pg. 82)

Hazing: Written on August 2, 2018 based on numerous reports of wildfires burning in California, including 12 active fiores as of August 2, 2018. Hazing is a practice of putting initiates through trials of physical endurance as a condition of entrance into a group. Many college campuses have hazing as a requirement for clubs. The practice has caused some deaths and thus become suspect. (Pg. 85)

The Life You Saved: Written in response to a writing prompt from James Lee Job: "Write as if you are speaking to the 16 year old you. What one thing would you tell yourself?" I had polio as a child and the March of Dimes helped take care of the treatment. It was a relatively mild case but did effect my left leg and hip with subsequent scoliosis, which has presented ongoing challenges. The residual effects of polio saved me from being drafted in the military during the Vietnam war even though my birthdate was #1 in the draft lottery. Also around age 16, I wanted to grow my hair long. Dad, the family barber, decided it was time to cut it. This led to a "battle of wills" and a rather severe beating. So, the poem to my younger self was a reframe of those events. (Pg. 86)

Waiting For A Ride: Written in December 2018 at a writing retreat with Roger Housden held at Spirit Rock, a Buddhist Retreat and learning center in Northern California. (Pg. 88)

A "Pinch Me" Moment: This was the first poem I wrote after *Gospel of Radiance.* I had decided to stop resisting religious or spiritual imagery in my writing. A "Pinch Me" Moment served as a kind of welcome for more spiritually oriented poems to come. (Pg. 93)

Jesus In A Hot Air Balloon: This was also among the first set of poems that I wrote after "opening the floodgates" for spiritual imagery. It was also the first poem that I wrote that referred directly to Jesus. (Pg. 94)

Man In The Moon: While writing *Man In The Moon*, I looked up images of Jesus holding up his fingers and learned that this is a blessing mudra and that his fingers also supposedly shape the letters of his name. (Pg. 95)

Buddha Came To Visit, Uninvited: Another poem that came to me as a piece. It explores some of the differences to me between Buddhism and Christianity. (Pg 96)

Hungry Ghosts: This poem is excerpted from a "letter to my future self" written on August 2, 2018 and read on August 15, 2019. When I compose a letter to the future, I consider holidays that fall on the desired dates. August 15, 2019, was considered by some to be the day of the Assumption of Mary. It was also the Ghost festival time (the day the gates of hell are opened and the dead are allowed to walk the earth in search of food) in Taiwan and likely China. (Pg. 97)

Jealous God: Written on January 20, 2019 at Asilomar after recognizing that I was jealous, or perhaps envious, of Micheal O'Sulleibahn. Michael is a long time friend of the famous poet, David Whyte, who has taken Micheal on as a poetry apprentice. I once asked David for mentoring on my poetry during a tour of Ireland and he refused. (Pg. 98)

Salt Pillar: This poem refers to the story of Lot's wife in Genesis. An angel of god appeared to Lot and commanded him to escape Sodom with his family and "not to look back." Lot had offered his daughters to appease God. Lot's wife looked back to see if they also escaped. When she did, she was immediately turned to stone as punishment. (Pg. 99)

Angels: I wrote *Angels* in 2007 and included it in a small chapbook, *Finding Family*, that I distributed to friends and family. (Pg. 100)

Mother Mary: After writing the initial line, "mornings are my niche," I looked up the word niche, which means a recess in a wall. That gave me the image of a small altar with a statue of Mother Mary. I looked up images of Mary and, in many, she is holding something in her hand. Here's what I wrote in my analysis after I finished *Mother Mary*: The narrator is: 1. one of the fallen? 2. is about to fall? 3. has some task or duty related to the fallen? 4. Other??? The vial is empty because 1. the narrator is too late; 2. he has already partaken of it? 3. The narrator must fill it (for example with tears of the fallen?). (Pg. 102)

Having A Beer With The Buddha: Christianity and Buddhism are the two religious systems with which I am most familiar. I do not follow either although I am much more inclined toward the openness and generosity of Buddhist philosophy and the practice of compassion than the exclusivity of the Christian faith. (Pg. 103)

Echo: Another poem based on myth of Narcissus and Echo. The word Narcissism, used to describe extreme vanity and self-centeredness, is derived from the myth. The story has always fascinated me because I am fairly self-centered, but hopefully not vain Echo loves Narcissus but has been condemned by the Gods to repeat what is said to her. Because of this, Narcissus rejected her. She then pined away until only her echoing voice remained. (Pg. 104)

The Master's Stick: This poem explores the idea of enlightenment, which is often depicted as a sudden event in Buddhist teaching tales. I have heard that some Buddhist masters use a stick to hit students when they lose concentration in meditation or as a teaching tool. (Pg. 105)

The Gospel of Radiance

Acknowledgments

The *Gospel of Radiance* would not have come into the light without the support and encouragement of many people. Let me first give a nod to the Sacramento Poetry Center (SPC) and the thriving poetry community in Sacramento, California, which offer me a venue and an audience to share and test my work. A special thanks goes to the facilitators of SPC's Marie Writer's Group, including Bob Stanley, Ann Michaels, Laura Rosenthal and Patricia Wentzel and to all the fellow participants in this ongoing group, who have inspired me by their writing and their response to my writing. And another special thanks goes to SPC's Tuesday Night Workshop facilitated by Danyen Powell and all those attendees who have offered valuable feedback on poems that I have "workshopped" with them.

I am especially indebted to my mentors and models in Poetry. A big thanks goes to Roger Housden, whose generative writing workshops have inspired lots of poems over the years and whose mentoring has helped sharpen my pen and tighten my script. I had the pleasure of attending the 2018-2019 year-long workshop with Mark Nepo. Mark's magical way of transforming experience into wisdom is a marvel and an inspiration. I want to thank all my cohorts in Mark Nepo's year long group who encouraged me to share some poetry with them along the way. My gratitude also goes out to David Whyte especially for his amazing ability to tell stories and speak poetry directly into the hearts and minds of his audience.

I have been blessed with a few staunch supporters of my work who have spread the word, including Stephen Gilligan, Judith Delozier,

Larry Dillenbeck, Tim and Kris Hallbom, and others. I am especially grateful to Robert Dilts who has shared my poems in workshops he conducts around the world. He has put me on the map as a poet in the hearts and minds of many people in many countries. A big thanks goes out to the many fans and students in my own classes who have enjoyed poems I've shared and found them helpful in their own journey in life. There are many others, to numerous to list here, who have served in my own personal journey to be a spirit in the world and live soulfully, which is the essential theme in all of my work. Thank you to all who have taught me, nurtured me, inspired me, and guided me.

Finally, I must make a deep bow of gratitude my muse: the angel of inspiration that so often speaks through me and never tires of the effort even when my words fall short of the feeling or fail to do justice to the sentiments of the soul. May the fountain continue to flow words to the page and onward to the eyes, ears, hearts, and minds of those who read them.

The Gospel of Radiance

About The Author

At times, people tell me that I have a "way with words" or a "gift" for poetry. Poetry, like so many of the creative arts, is a bridge between willful effort and intuitive access. There is a kernel of natural ability for me and I have enjoyed playing with words throughout my life, but I have also honed my language skills and crafted my poetic expression for years. I have worked actively with the language of change for over 35 years in my career as a hypnotherapist and Neuro-Linguistic Programming (NLP) practitioner and trainer. I have practiced and tested language patterns with clients and students and gradually developed skills that transferred directly into writing and speaking poetry.

What may seem a "gift" now has been a labor of love over many years. It was a labor that I did not know I would apply to poetry in those years of dedicated effort. I wrote poetry as a teenager and a few times during my adult and middle years, but only began to write poetry in earnest starting around the year 2000. I began sharing poetry in classes in 2001 and immediately felt it resonated for me and with my audiences.

Although I have worked to develop my craft, I'm also acutely aware that poetry is a "gift." There is more than "me" in the writing of poetry. Like so many creative arts, poetry lies at the edge of self. Many people know the word "inspiration" means "to breathe in," but few realize it comes from the Greek idea that Apollo, the god of music and poetry, was "breathing in" to you and through you. My personal experience with hypnosis and working with the unconscious has paid off in helping me to cross the bridge into the unknown, to open myself to being inspired, and to find my way back with this "gift."

I have shared poems in NLP, Coaching, and Hypnosis workshops around the world for many years and my poetry has been translated into Chinese, French, German, Italian, Spanish, and other languages. I have previously published seven books of poetry: Heaven In Our Hearts (2012); Endless Horizon (2013); Divine Whispering (2014); The Poetry of Life (2015); The Work of Being Yourself (2016); Falling Before Grace (2017); and Bearing Witness (2018). My home town of Sacramento, California has a very active art scene and a thriving poetry community, including the Sacramento Poetry Center (SPC), of which I am a member. The SPC celebrated its 40th anniversary in 2019.

For info on booking, contact Nick at:

Nick LeForce
Inner Works
www.nickleforce.com
nickleforce@me.com
+1 916-622-2980

If you enjoyed The Gospel of Radiance, you will also like my other books of poetry, available through amazon.com in physical form or at nickleforce.com where some are available in downloadable digital format or as audio books.

Heaven In Our Hearts

These poems will truly lead you to an encounter with that other version of yourself that lives and loves freely and onward into the life you were meant to live.

Endless Horizon

These poems will expand your horizon—that point that limits the potential and defines the probable in your life—allowing you to see, for yourself, all things possible and bring the gifts inside of you to the outside world.

Divine Whispering

These poems invite you to hear the divine whispering to you, challenge you to live soulfully in the world, and encourage you to engage in a deeper, more profound relationship with life.

The Poetry of Life

This collection of pictures and poems demonstrates how to word the world in a way that brings you to life and life to you. The Poetry of Life teaches how to create empowered contexts for cultivating your wisdom and bringing out the best in yourself and others.

The Work of Being Your Self
Navigating The 5 Dynamic Dilemmas

More than a book of poetry, the Work of Being Your Self uses poetry, questions to explore, and writing prompts to support the reader in navigating five "dynamic dilemmas" of life, which are archetypal conflicts that we must revisit from time to time throughout life: Safety and Risk, Head and Heart, Fight and Flow, Self and Others, Here and There,

Falling Before Grace

This book of love poems combines three previously published e-books that were written for Valentine's day (2014: Turn Towards Love; 2015: At First Sight; & 2016: A Season of Longing) into one physical book. A perfect gift for Valentine's day or for lover's at any time.

Bearing Witness

Bearing Witness is a book of poetry based on a 5-step method of the process I use for writing and that I believe serves as a method for a transforming experience into wisdom: Presence, Engagement, Reflection, Cultivation, and Expression.

The Gospel of Radiance

Made in the USA
San Bernardino, CA
01 December 2019